FOCUS ON ENDANGERED SPECIES
ENDANGERED BIRDS

by Laura Stickney

BrightPoint Press

San Diego, CA

© 2024 BrightPoint Press
an imprint of ReferencePoint Press, Inc.
Printed in the United States

For more information, contact:
BrightPoint Press
PO Box 27779
San Diego, CA 92198
www.BrightPointPress.com

ALL RIGHTS RESERVED.

No part of this work covered by the copyright hereon may be reproduced or used in any form or by any means—graphic, electronic, or mechanical, including photocopying, recording, taping, web distribution, or information storage retrieval systems—without the written permission of the publisher.

LIBRARY OF CONGRESS CATALOGING-IN-PUBLICATION DATA

Names: Stickney, Laura, author.
Title: Endangered birds / by Laura Stickney.
Description: San Diego, CA: BrightPoint, [2024] | Series: Focus on endangered species | Includes bibliographical references and index. | Audience: Ages 13 | Audience: Grades 7-9
Identifiers: LCCN 2023000089 (print) | LCCN 2023000090 (eBook) | ISBN 9781678206420 (hardcover) | ISBN 9781678206437 (eBook)
Subjects: LCSH: Rare birds--Juvenile literature. | Endangered species--Juvenile literature. | Birds--Conservation--Juvenile literature. | California condor--Conservation--Juvenile literature. | African penguin--Conservation--Juvenile literature. | Kakapo--Conservation--Juvenile literature. | Lear's macaw--Conservation--Juvenile literature.
Classification: LCC QL676.7 .S68 2024 (print) | LCC QL676.7 (eBook) | DDC 598.168--dc23/eng/20230112
LC record available at https://lccn.loc.gov/2023000089
LC eBook record available at https://lccn.loc.gov/2023000090

CONTENTS

AT A GLANCE	4
INTRODUCTION **SAVING A SCAVENGER**	6
CHAPTER ONE **CALIFORNIA CONDORS**	12
CHAPTER TWO **AFRICAN PENGUINS**	24
CHAPTER THREE **KAKAPO**	36
CHAPTER FOUR **LEAR'S MACAWS**	46
Glossary	58
Source Notes	59
For Further Research	60
Index	62
Image Credits	63
About the Author	64

AT A GLANCE

- In 2021, almost 1,500 bird species were threatened with extinction. Pollution, habitat loss, climate change, and more put these birds at risk.

- California condors eat carrion. When hunters use lead bullets to shoot animals, condors can eat pieces of lead and get lead poisoning.

- Conservationists have raised many condors and released them back into the wild.

- The biggest threats to African penguins are overfishing and global warming.

- Conservationists help protect African penguins. They rehabilitate injured or sick penguins, lead oil spill rescues, and monitor penguin colonies.

- Kakapo are flightless parrots native to New Zealand. Early European settlers introduced invasive species such as rats, cats, and stoats into kakapo habitats. These predators ate kakapo eggs and chicks.

- Kakapo have low genetic diversity and don't breed often. Conservationists work to keep their population steady. They guard against predators, provide food, and do health checks.

- Lear's macaws live in the Caatinga region of northeastern Brazil. Poachers often capture them for the pet trade. Deforestation and land clearing also harm the macaws' habitat.

- Government protections and wildlife trade bans help protect Lear's macaws and their habitat.

INTRODUCTION

SAVING A SCAVENGER

It's a bright morning in California. A huge bird soars over the forest. She's a California condor. This species is the biggest wild bird in North America. Her powerful wings stretch 9 feet (2.7 m). She scans the ground below for food.

Finally, she spots a dead deer. This may seem gross. But for the condor, it's lunch. She's a scavenger. She eats carrion, or dead animals. The condor swoops down to eat. However, this deer is dangerous.

The California condor can fly at more than 55 miles per hour (89 kmh).

It was killed by a lead bullet. Lead is a toxic metal. Many hunters shoot animals with lead bullets. These bullets break into pieces and get stuck inside the animal's body. When the condor eats the deer, she eats the toxic pieces. Soon, she grows weak and her wings droop. She has lead poisoning.

    Luckily, the condor has been tagged. She has a radio transmitter on her wing. This helps **conservationists** find her. Conservationists work to protect wildlife and the environment. They find high levels of lead in the condor's blood. They bring her to a zoo for treatment. The treatment uses

Conservationists place radio transmitters with numbered tags on condors to easily identify each bird.

special drugs to remove the lead. It's a long, difficult process. But after a few months, the condor gets healthier. She can return to the wild.

BIRDS ON THE BRINK

Many condors are treated for lead poisoning. But many die from it too. In 2020, lead poisoning caused half of all wild California condor deaths. It's one reason condors are an endangered species. This means they're at risk of going extinct in the wild. In 2021, almost 1,500 bird species were endangered or vulnerable.

Many birds today are threatened by pollution, habitat loss, **climate change**, hunting, and more. But people can help endangered birds. They can learn more

Conservation, education, and responsible tourism are all ways to protect endangered birds.

about birds and work to protect them through conservation, advocating for legal protections, and fighting poaching. This way, they can help birds survive and thrive.

1
CALIFORNIA CONDORS

California condors fly for hours without flapping their wings. They soar hundreds of miles searching for carrion. Condors are vultures. They don't kill animals. They eat only dead things. Many eat dead deer or cattle. Others eat dead whales or sea lions. This food is messy.

But a condor's features keep the bird clean. Its beak easily tears flesh. Its featherless head keeps carrion from getting stuck on the condor.

California condors are known for their red eyes.

Millions of years ago, condors lived throughout North America. They ate the bodies of mammals such as mammoths. When those animals died out, condors had less food. Their **range** got smaller. By the 1800s, condors lived in only a few parts of the western United States.

CLEANING THE ECOSYSTEM

Eating carrion sounds dirty. But carrion birds are important to the ecosystem. Rotting carcasses can spread harmful bacteria. This can make animals and humans sick. By eating carrion, condors keep landscapes clean. Their digestive systems break down bacteria in corpses. This prevents diseases from spreading.

Throughout the 1800s and 1900s, their population fell. Early settlers hunted in the condor's range. Sometimes the settlers shot condors. They also used lead bullets to hunt other animals. The bullets poisoned the carrion the condors ate. By 1987, only twenty-seven condors were alive in zoos. None were left in the wild.

LETHAL LEAD BULLETS

Lead bullets are the biggest threat to condors. Many hunters still use these bullets. The bullets leave bits of lead in the dead animals. This is dangerous for condors. Tiana Williams-Clausen is a wildlife biologist. She says that when it comes to lead, "a piece as small as the head of a pin is enough to kill a condor."[1]

The condor's digestive system absorbs lead quickly. Lead gets into its blood and bones. It gives the condor lead poisoning. Lead poisoning shuts down a condor's organs. Sick condors can't care for their chicks. This is a problem because condors lay an egg only every other year. Uncared-for chicks die. This causes the condor population to fall.

California condors build nests in caves on cliffs.

Since 1999, hundreds of condors have had lead poisoning.

A POISONOUS PROBLEM

DDT also harms condors. DDT is a chemical that was invented in the 1940s.

While DDT was banned in the United States, some countries still use it to prevent mosquito-borne illnesses.

It was used to kill pests. DDT harms humans and animals. The United States banned DDT in 1972. But it lasts a long time in the environment. Between the 1940s and the 1970s, DDT was dumped off coasts.

Many marine animals that condors eat still carry traces of it.

DDT makes condor eggs have thin shells. The eggs break more easily. They're 20 to 40 percent less likely to hatch.

CONDOR CONSERVATION

In 1982, conservationists started a captive breeding program for condors. The US Fish and Wildlife Service worked with zoos in California. They took condors from the wild and moved them to zoos. Condor eggs were also taken to zoos. The first chick bred in **captivity** hatched in 1988. In 1992, the first captive-bred condors returned to the wild. The program breeds about thirty chicks each year.

Conservationists track condors in the wild. They put ID tags and radio transmitters on their wings. Conservationists track condors for many reasons. The scientists feed the birds until they can hunt on

SACRED SCAVENGERS

The Yurok tribe has lived in northwestern California for centuries. Condors appear in Yurok stories and ceremonies. They symbolize renewal and balance. Condors were missing from northwestern California for many years. That changed in 2022 when the Yurok Condor Restoration Program released four into the area.

their own. They also clear trash from nests. They even check on the chicks. Every year, condors are captured for medical testing. Experts check for lead poisoning.

Thanks to conservation work, the condor population has grown. There were more than 500 condors in 2020. This included 200 in the wild. By 2022, more than 300 condors were flying free.

FIGHTING AGAINST LEAD

Lead poisoning is still an issue. In 2007, California's governor signed a bill to fight this problem. The bill banned using lead bullets for hunting in parts of California. But condors fly long distances. They could still fly to places with unsafe carrion. Conservationists called for a bigger ban. In 2019, it became illegal for hunters to use lead bullets anywhere in California. Hunters who used them would be fined.

Some hunters were unhappy about this. Lead bullets are cheaper than non-lead bullets. Many hunters didn't want to pay more. Some people worry hunters will keep using lead bullets illegally. Education can help fix this. Some conservationists educate hunters about lead bullets.

Lead isn't the only pollution that kills condors. Eating microtrash is the leading cause of death for California condor chicks.

Others offer perks to hunters who switch to non-lead bullets.

2
AFRICAN PENGUINS

African penguins live in colonies off Africa's southwestern coast. They're known for their donkey-like noises. Waterproof feathers keep them warm while swimming. The penguins also have unique markings. Pink patches of skin above their eyes keep them cool. When penguins get hot, blood flows to these patches to release body heat. African penguins live on rocky beaches. They hunt for fish offshore. The penguins are skilled swimmers. They can dive up to 400 feet (120 m).

African penguins mate for life. They form close bonds with their partners.

GREEDY FOR GUANO

In the 1800s, there were about 1.5 million African penguins. But the population quickly fell. Penguin eggs were a popular food. Between 1900 and 1930, people stole 13 million eggs from one colony. They also took guano from nesting sites. Guano is bird poop. It builds up in thick

WHITE GOLD

In the 1800s and 1900s, guano was a popular trade product. Human-made fertilizers hadn't been invented yet. But guano helped crops grow. So many people wanted guano that it became known as white gold. People mined it from penguin nesting sites. Today, guano collecting is illegal.

layers on rocks. Penguins make nests with it. Guano protects eggs from predators, storms, and extreme temperatures.

People use guano for fertilizer. Between 1841 and 1983, people took 2 million tons (1.8 million metric tons) of guano from nesting sites. Without guano, penguins had to build nests in the open. Eggs and chicks were less protected.

PEOPLE AND POLLUTION

One of the biggest threats to penguins is the fishing industry. Penguins eat sardines and anchovies. These nutritious fish keep

African penguin couples take turns sitting on their eggs.

penguins healthy. But humans also eat them. Companies overfish near penguin colonies. This leaves fewer fish for penguins to eat. Penguins must swim farther away to find food or eat less nutritious fish.

According to marine biologist Lorien Pichegru, this is one way overfishing harms oceans. She says fish such as sardines and anchovies "are the cornerstones of our oceans . . . and their overfishing is the greatest threat currently faced by seabirds."[2]

Humans disrupt penguins in other ways too. Tourists sometimes get too close to penguins. This causes them stress. Other penguins get tangled in trash or hit by cars. Oil tankers often sail past penguin colonies. Other companies drill for oil nearby. Both of these activities can cause oil spills. Oil makes it hard for the penguins' feathers to

The African penguin takes oil from a gland near its tail and spreads it over its feathers. This is called preening. Preening keeps the penguin's feathers clean and waterproof.

keep their bodies warm. If they try to clean their feathers, they may eat the oil and be poisoned.

WARMING WATERS

Meanwhile, climate change causes extreme weather around penguin colonies. Hotter temperatures, heavy rain, and storms can harm nests. Oceans are getting warmer too. Warming waters have made the fish that penguins hunt move farther away.

This lack of food disrupts penguin molting cycles. During molting, penguins lose their feathers and grow new ones. They need feathers to stay warm while swimming. This means they shouldn't hunt or swim during molting. They usually stay on land until new feathers grow. Before molting,

African penguin chicks rely on their parents for food for two to four months.

penguins usually eat more food to fatten up. But they can't do this when there aren't enough fish. This means many penguins must start hunting before their feathers grow back. This is dangerous. Swimming in cold water can harm molting penguins.

Sometimes chicks hatch when their parents are molting. Their parents are unable to feed them. This leaves many chicks abandoned and hungry.

PROTECTING PENGUINS

In 2021, there were fewer than 20,000 breeding pairs of African penguins. But conservation groups are working to raise this number. One South African group **rehabilitates** injured and sick African penguins. It rescues about 1,000 penguins each year. It has also raised 7,000 chicks since 2006. Before releasing penguins, conservationists put trackers on them. This helps the conservationists keep penguins healthy. The group also leads oil spill rescues and education programs.

Many conservationists say fishing bans are needed near penguin colonies. Bans could help penguin populations grow. But some people oppose bans. Fishing companies provide jobs and money for

ECOTOURISM

Tourists can harm penguins. But **ecotourism** helps raise awareness about them. In South Africa, tourism at a single penguin colony brings in $19.5 million annually. Visitors can see penguins up close. Money from this tourism helps fund penguin conservation.

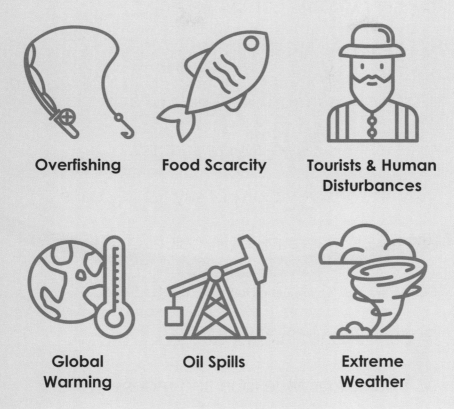

African penguins face a variety of threats, including human disturbances, global warming, and oil spills. The biggest danger is overfishing.

the area's economy. Conservationists are working with fishing companies to find a solution.

3
KAKAPO

Kakapo are the world's heaviest parrots. They are also the only flightless parrots. Kakapo are covered in green feathers. They have round faces and bulky bodies. This is why they're sometimes called owl parrots. Kakapo are nocturnal. At night, they forage for flowers, fruits, and seeds. They climb trees with their feet and use their wings for balance. Kakapo breed only when rimu trees bear fruit. This only happens every two to four years.

Kakapo have one of the longest lifespans of any bird. It is estimated that they can live up to ninety years.

ISLAND INVADERS

For centuries, kakapo lived throughout New Zealand. Kakapo freeze when they sense danger. This helps them blend in with trees. They do this to hide from predators. But in the 1300s, humans arrived. Slow-moving kakapo were easy targets for hunters and hunting dogs. The Maori people often used them for meat and feathers.

In the 1800s, European settlers introduced **invasive species** into the kakapo's habitat. Rats, cats, and stoats arrived on settlers' ships. These new predators ate kakapo chicks and eggs.

Kakapo don't swallow the plants they eat. Instead, they chew the food, suck out the nutrients, and leave the chewed plant matter behind.

The kakapo population quickly fell. By 1995, only fifty-one kakapo were still alive.

In the 1980s and 1990s, conservationists moved all kakapo to protected islands. But invasive species still threaten them. Female kakapo raise chicks alone. They often leave their nests to find food. This leaves nests unprotected from rats and stoats. Predators target adult kakapo too. A study in the 1990s found that on one island, cats killed more than half the adult kakapo population each year.

A SPECIES IN DANGER

The kakapo population is very small. This leads many kakapo to mate with relatives.

Kakapo are very friendly. Some even try to preen humans.

This is called inbreeding. Inbreeding causes kakapo to have very similar genetics. This makes it harder for kakapo to have chicks. Studies show that only about half of kakapo eggs are fertile. Inbreeding also makes kakapo more vulnerable to disease.

Conservation biologist Andrew Digby works for New Zealand's Kakapo Recovery Team. He explains why having similar genetics can be so dangerous. Different genetics make animals susceptible to different diseases. Digby says that if a disease comes along that kakapo genetics are susceptible to, "the entire population will be in danger of being wiped out."[3]

KAKAPO CONSERVATION

The Kakapo Recovery Team manages the kakapo population. The team uses traps and technology to keep the kakapo's

Kakapo's favorite food is rimu berries. When rimu trees bear fruit, kakapo barely eat anything else.

islands predator-free. In 2016, the government started Predator Free 2050. This plan aims to get rid of all invasive predators in New Zealand by 2050.

The team also carefully monitors kakapo on the islands. Kakapo carry radio transmitters on their backs. These collect data about the birds' health, locations, and mating habits. Conservationists also monitor nests and do annual health checks.

BOOSTING THE POPULATION

The Kakapo Recovery Team has several strategies to help boost the kakapo population. Part of their job includes setting up feeding stations. These help the kakapo eat enough during breeding season.

Meanwhile, scientists study kakapo genetics. They figure out which birds should mate to produce the healthiest chicks. This has been very successful. During the 2022 breeding season, the population grew from 197 to 252. This was the biggest kakapo population in almost fifty years.

SOCIAL MEDIA SUPERSTAR

In 2009, a nature documentary featured a spunky kakapo. His name was Sirocco. He became an internet sensation and was named the official "spokesbird" for New Zealand conservation. The Kakapo Recovery Team uses social media to raise awareness about kakapo. They share updates and kakapo-themed memes on Sirocco's Facebook page. Sirocco has more than 230,000 followers.

4
LEAR'S MACAWS

Lear's macaws have bright blue feathers and yellow chins. They live in the Caatinga region of northeastern Brazil. This is a dry forest region with thorny trees, shrubs, and cacti. Lear's macaws nest on sandstone cliffs. Their hooked beaks help them crack open seeds and fruit.

They mainly eat Licurí palm nuts. Lear's macaws eat up to 350 Licurí nuts every day. While eating, they scatter nuts on the ground. This plants new palms.

Lear's macaws are curious and playful.

DEFORESTATION DANGERS

Lear's macaws were discovered in 1978. Their population fell during the following years. One reason for this is the loss of their habitat. Lear's macaws rely on Licurí palms for food. These palms once covered about 96,500 square miles (250,000 sq km). But much of this land has been cleared. The logging industry cuts down trees. Plants are cleared to make room for farms.

    Some farmers also use harmful land-clearing methods. They burn trees down. This harms the soil. Others let livestock graze on Caatinga land.

The Caatinga region of Brazil hosts more than 500 species of birds.

This makes it hard for trees to regrow. At least 50 percent of the macaws' habitat has been harmed.

When Licurí palms are cut down, macaws have less food. Biologist Bernardo Ortiz-von Halle explains, "A decrease in food sources . . . has brought the macaws into

Wind turbines kill hundreds of thousands of birds and bats every year.

conflict with local farmers as they now feed on corn crops."[4] When macaws eat crops, sometimes farmers shoot them.

WIND FARM WORRIES

Another threat to the macaws was an energy company. It planned to build a wind farm in the Caatinga. The company began clearing land in the area without permission.

In 2021, Brazil's government ordered the company to pause. But the company continued the project. Many people worry that wind turbines and electricity lines will be a danger to the macaws.

POACHING AND THE PET TRADE

Poaching is another danger. Throughout history, people have wanted macaws as pets. They admired the birds' colorful feathers and speaking abilities. Because of this, Lear's macaws were targeted by poachers. Poaching is when someone illegally captures, sells, or kills wildlife. Poachers smuggle macaws and sell them as pets. Some people will pay thousands of dollars for a Lear's macaw.

WILDLIFE TRADE BANS

Many governments have wildlife trade bans. These make it illegal to traffic endangered species. The US Wild Bird Act bans the import of many endangered birds. Bans help prevent poaching. But many conservationists say new strategies are needed to stop poaching completely.

Bird poaching remains a problem in Brazil. One study looked at which animals were smuggled the most. Between 2012 and 2015, more than 90 percent of reported poachers were smuggling birds. A 2020 report studied **wildlife trafficking** in Brazil. It found that the bird trade affects about 400 species in the country. Lear's macaws are often easy poaching targets. They have a small range. This makes them easy to find.

Poaching takes Lear's macaws away from their natural habitats. They're unable to breed with their mates or care for chicks.

This harms the Caatinga ecosystem too. Without Lear's macaws to spread seeds, the forest can't regrow.

SAVING LEAR'S MACAWS

Conservationists work with Brazil's government to protect Lear's macaws. In 2022, most Lear's macaws lived in two colonies. Both are recognized by the

THE POET'S PARROT

Lear's macaws are named after British poet and illustrator Edward Lear. In 1832, Lear published a book of parrot paintings. One painting showed a blue macaw. People thought it was a hyacinth macaw. Later, experts realized it was a new species. They named it after Lear.

Alliance for Zero Extinction (AZE). AZE protects important sites for at-risk species. Placing protections on the macaws' habitat helps prevent deforestation.

Conservation centers also support Lear's macaws. Most macaws live near Canudos Biological Station. This was built to monitor macaws in the wild. It supports conservation projects. It also has programs for ecotourists and birdwatchers. Other centers run captive breeding programs. Conservationists raise captive-bred macaws and macaws rescued from poachers. Released macaws are tagged with trackers and microchips. Poachers are less likely to steal tagged macaws.

Many conservation centers work with the community. Some hire locals as tour guides or poaching guards. This provides jobs for people. It keeps them from working as land-clearers. Locals also help replant Licurí palms. Other conservationists work with farmers. One group began giving farmers corn to replace crops eaten by macaws. This makes farmers less likely to shoot the birds.

Conservation helps save endangered birds from extinction. But many birds are

Lear's macaws are known to mimic human voices. However, their voices sound scratchy and hoarse.

still at risk. Luckily, people don't have to be conservationists to help. Anyone can make a difference. They can keep the environment clean. They can hunt with non-lead bullets. Even small steps can help protect birds in need.

GLOSSARY

captivity
when an animal is raised, kept, or bred in a zoo or other enclosure outside of the wild

climate change
long-term changes in global temperature and weather patterns

conservationists
people who work toward the protection and preservation of natural environments, plants, and wildlife

ecotourism
tourism that is focused on seeing wildlife and supporting conservation

invasive species
a species that isn't native to a specific environment

range
the geographic area or region where an animal can be found

rehabilitates
treats a sick or injured wild animal until it can be released back into the wild

wildlife trafficking
the illegal capture, trade, and sale of wild animals

SOURCE NOTES

CHAPTER ONE: CALIFORNIA CONDORS

1. Quoted in Aaron Scott, "The Quest to Save the California Condor," *NPR*, June 28, 2022. www.npr.org.

CHAPTER TWO: AFRICAN PENGUINS

2. Quoted in Jaco Prinsloo, "The African Penguin's Last Stronghold," *Earth Island Journal*, May 12, 2021. www.earthisland.org.

CHAPTER THREE: KAKAPO

3. Quoted in Tammana Begum, "New Zealand's Quirky Kakapo Are Pulled Back from the Edge of Extinction," *Natural History Museum London*, n.d. www.nhm.ac.uk.

CHAPTER FOUR: LEAR'S MACAWS

4. Bernardo Ortiz-von Halle, "Bird's-Eye View: Lessons from 50 Years of Bird Trade Regulation and Conservation in Amazon Countries," *Traffic*, January 16, 2019. www.traffic.org.

FOR FURTHER RESEARCH

BOOKS

Sandra Markle, *The Great Penguin Rescue: Saving the African Penguins*. Minneapolis, MN: Millbrook Press, 2018.

Joyce Markovics, *Kakapos*. Ann Arbor, MI: Cherry Lake Publishing, 2021.

Sy Montgomery, *Condor Comeback*. Boston, MA: Houghton Mifflin Harcourt, 2020.

INTERNET SOURCES

"African Penguin," *San Diego Zoo Wildlife Alliance: Animals and Plants*, n.d. https://animals.sandiegozoo.org.

"California Condor," *American Bird Conservancy*, n.d. https://abcbirds.org.

"Kakapo Behavior," *New Zealand Department of Conservation*, n.d. www.doc.govt.nz.

WEBSITES

American Bird Conservancy
https://abcbirds.org

The American Bird Conservancy works to support bird conservation and protect important bird habitats in the Americas.

National Audubon Society
www.audubon.org

The National Audubon Society is a nonprofit organization dedicated to protecting and celebrating birds. It works to educate people about birds, protect habitats, and support bird conservation.

The IUCN Red List of Threatened Species
www.iucnredlist.org

The International Union for Conservation of Nature (IUCN) Red List documents the official statuses of threatened species around the world. Governments and wildlife organizations use the list to determine what conservation actions are needed to protect wildlife.

INDEX

Africa, 24
African penguins, 24–35

beaks, 13, 46
Brazil, 46, 51, 53
breeding programs, 19–20, 45, 55

California condors, 6–10, 12–23
carrion, 7, 12–13, 14, 15, 22
chicks, 16, 19–20, 21, 27, 33, 38, 40–41, 45, 53
climate change, 10, 31, 35
conservationists, 8, 19–21, 22–23, 33–35, 40, 42–45, 52, 54–57

DDT, 17–19
diseases, 14, 41–42

eggs, 16, 19, 26, 27, 38, 41

feathers, 13, 24, 29–30, 31–32, 36, 38, 46, 52
fishing, 27–29, 34–35

guano, 26–27

habitat loss, 10, 48–49, 55
hunting, 8, 10, 15, 22–23, 38

inbreeding, 41
invasive species, 38, 40, 43

kakapo, 36–45

lead bullets, 8, 15–16, 21–23, 57
Lear's macaws, 46–56

molting, 31–33

nests, 21, 26–27, 31, 40, 44, 46
New Zealand, 38, 42–43, 45
North America, 6, 14

poaching, 11, 51–53, 55–56
pollution, 10, 21, 29
populations, 15, 16, 21, 26, 34, 39, 40, 42, 44, 45, 48
predators, 27, 38, 40, 43

radio transmitters, 8, 20, 44
ranges, 14, 15, 53

scavenging, 7
social media, 45
swimming, 24–25, 28, 31–32

tourism, 34

US Fish and Wildlife Service, 19

wind turbines, 51
wings, 6, 8, 12, 20, 37

Yurok tribe, 20

zoos, 8, 15, 19

IMAGE CREDITS

Cover: © Aqua Images/Shutterstock Images
5: © Lubos Chlubny/Shutterstock Images
7: © Brian A Wolf/Shutterstock Images
9: © Eric Dale/Shutterstock Images
11: © NicolasMcComber/iStockphoto
13: © Infiniumguy/Shutterstock Images
17: © Joseph Brandt/USFWS
18: © GrooTrai/Shutterstock Images
23: © Doble-d/iStockphoto
25: © Sergey Uryadnikov/Shutterstock Images
28: © Simon Eeman/Shutterstock Images
30: © Roger Utting/Shutterstock Images
32: © Niall Dunne/Shutterstock Images
35 (top left, top middle, top right): © Alex Blogoodf/Shutterstock Images
35 (bottom left, bottom middle, bottom right): © Picture Window/Shutterstock Images
37: © Liu Yang/iStockphoto
39: © Tui De Roy/Nature Picture Library/Alamy
41: © Jake Osborne/Flickr
43: © Brent Stephenson/Nature Picture Library/Alamy
47: © Agami Photo Agency/Shutterstock Images
49: © Cacio Murilo/Shutterstock Images
50: © Fokke Baarssen/Shutterstock Images
57: © TacioPhilip/iStockphoto

ABOUT THE AUTHOR

Laura Stickney is a writer, editor, and artist from the Twin Cities area in Minnesota. She is currently pursuing a master of fine arts degree in creative writing.